DECORATIVE ALPHABETS
THROUGHOUT THE AGES

INTRODUCTION BY

PAT RUSSELL

FELLOW OF THE SOCIETY OF SCRIBES
AND ILLUMINATORS

CRESCENT BOOKS

NEW YORK

PUBLISHED BY CRESCENT BOOKS
DISTRIBUTED BY CROWN PUBLISHERS, INC.
225 PARK AVENUE SOUTH
NEW YORK, NEW YORK 10003

MANY OF THE PLATES IN THIS BOOK ARE REPRODUCED
FROM NINETEENTH CENTURY ART MANUALS.
THE COLOURS USED MAY THEREFORE DIFFER
FROM THOSE OF THE ORIGINAL MANUSCRIPTS.

POSTER ART SERIES

DECORATIVE ALPHABETS THROUGHOUT THE AGES
IS A VOLUME IN THE POSTER ART
SERIES. UP TO TEN PLATES MAY BE
REPRODUCED IN ANY ONE PROJECT OR
PUBLICATION, WITHOUT SPECIAL PERMISSION
AND FREE OF CHARGE. WHEREVER POSSIBLE THE
AUTHOR, TITLE AND PUBLISHER SHOULD BE ACKNOWLEDGED
IN A CREDIT NOTE. FOR PERMISSION TO MAKE MORE EXTENSIVE USE
OF THE PLATES IN THIS BOOK APPLICATION
MUST BE MADE TO THE PUBLISHER.

ISBN 0 517 66118 7

PRINTED IN ITALY

h g f e d c b a

INTRODUCTION

Decorative lettering has been in use from as early as the sixth century A.D., and has been practised with many variations throughout the ages to survive as a flourishing art form today. The endless decorative possibilities of letters have always fascinated artists and the plates in this book show examples of a wide variety of alphabets showing pattern work including all-over patterns, borders, in-filling designs, floral motifs, geometric and abstract patterns, scroll work and flourishes.

The letters we use today derive from a single source – the very fine and sophisticated capital letter developed by the Romans in the first century A.D. (plate 34 shows its use by a modern artist). At this early date all writing was in capital letters; but later, when the spread of Christianity brought about an increasing demand for books, the consequent necessity of speeding up the writing process led to the evolvement in the ninth and tenth centuries of a second alphabet of small or lower case letters. This was used for the text of books, the capitals being reserved for headings and paragraph openings.

Man's desire to decorate his writing is age-old; until the sixth century, however, this was achieved only by variations in the size and colour of the letters. From then onwards until the introduction of printing in the sixteenth century, the art of the illuminated manuscript flourished throughout Europe. Sometimes the decorative effect was achieved by a controlled distortion and manipulation of the letters themselves; as, for example, in the early Anglo-Saxon manuscripts (plate 1). At other times, letters were formed from mysterious animals and fish, their attenuated forms writhing and turning in complex interlacing patterns. This is mostly associated with the major illuminations of the Anglo-Saxon period, but the use of animals and grotesques persisted well into later centuries (plates 2, 3, 5, 20 and 31); even today one can find letters incorporating animal and human forms.

During the tenth century a freer form of the Roman letter was developed characterized by swelling curves and marked contrast between the thick and thin strokes. It lent itself to elegant and restrained decoration (plate 4) and was used to mark the beginning of paragraphs or verses; hence it came to be known as a versal. Later, its curves and contrasts became more exaggerated and it lost its classical proportions to become what is called a Lombardic capital (plates 6, 9). Its bulky form, however, made it an ideal vehicle for ornamentation and, until the Renaissance, it was on this style of letter that most illuminated initials were based.

The historicism of the Renaissance also had its influence in the field of lettering, especially in Italy. The classical Roman letter, with its round 'O's and stately proportions, reflecting so closely the architecture of the Renaissance, once more became the accepted letterform and was used extensively in the Italian manuscripts of the fifteenth and sixteenth centuries (plates 14, 15, 19). In Northern Europe, however, the Lombardic letter was retained, together with a decorative pen-made Gothic capital (plates 11, 13).

Books, whether written and illuminated by hand or mass-produced by the printing press, have always been closely associated with education. In Anglo-Saxon times this was entirely the province of the monasteries and it was in these communities that Europe's earliest books were produced. The monks enriched their holy books with decoration as naturally as they would adorn their altars and shrines. The intricate patterns of interlacing animals and birds could not but reflect this spirituality since the work was part of a way of life devoted to the praise and glory of God. The monks used no gold, but their imagination, attention to detail, and sensitive use of colour resulted in major works of art that have rarely been surpassed.

An important feature of this period is the prolific use of tiny red dots to outline both the letters and decorative motifs. These help to integrate the artwork with its page and text, and serve the same function as do the filigree lines and curlicues in later manuscripts.

Between the sixth and ninth centuries monasteries throughout Europe, in Ireland, England, France, Germany, Spain and Italy, were busy transcribing the Gospels and other instructional books. Since distances were great and communications difficult, great variations in style developed simultaneously in the different countries. Charlemagne, when crowned Emperor of Europe in 800 A.D., decided to rectify this and called in Alcuin of York to advise him on the standardization of letterforms. As happened later in the Renaissance period, the decision was made to revert to the simple, clear and elegant forms of the early Roman capital, and to use a lower case letter that was based on the same classical proportions. It is interesting to note that basically these forms of letter have persisted until the present day. Decoration also took on a more classical character, using formalized acanthus leaves and other floral forms. Strange beasts were still in evidence, though not in such convoluted forms as in the Celtic work. These characteristics are typical of what is known as the Romanesque period.

The demand for books continued to grow when the universities rather than the Church became established as seats of learning, and the making of books passed gradually from the monasteries into the hands of secular scribes. These itinerant artists had as their patrons rich and powerful noblemen, and it was not long before their books were being designed to reflect the wealth of their employers rather than the glory of God. Gold was much used with more and more ornate decoration, and the formal motifs of the Romanesque period were superseded in the thirteenth and fourteenth centuries by more exuberant and naturalistic floral forms. Letters were filled with entwined vine-like patterns and surrounded by a plethora of tendrils, flourishes and curlicues (plates 8, 9), and burnished gold leaf was used abundantly, both as a background and for the letters themselves. The wide and bulbous shape of the Lombardic capital allowed plenty of space in the letter itself for all kinds of decoration; intricate geometric and abstract patterns, floral motifs, and counterchange designs. This letter in its turn was set in a richly ornate rectangle and the whole surrounded by a delicate filigree border.

In the late fourteenth and fifteenth centuries the spaces inside the letters, or counters, came to be used more for illustration (plate 12), and eventually, by the sixteenth century, the pictorial miniature surrounded by an ornate border superseded the large illuminated initial in the decoration of books. This development together with the invention of printing in 1453 brought about the decline of the illuminated letter as it had to make way for new needs and techniques. At first the printers, with the image of the illuminated page fresh in their minds, attempted to imitate the illuminated manuscript by the use of hand-painted initials. The large number of books now being produced, however, soon made this an impractical and, as early as 1457, decorative initials were being printed from wood blocks. These were often enriched with hand-colouring, but wood block printing in two colours was soon to follow.

This new technique brought about a complete change in the character of the decorative letter. The woodcut by its very nature produced strong contrasts of black and white and the possibility of fine white detailing, resulting in the production of white letters on a patterned black background. Renaissance influences still prevailed in the shape of the letters and their decoration, based on floral, animal and human forms (plates 18, 19, 20); but the sixteenth century shook off this influence and was a period of great imagination in the design of initial letters for use in printing (plates 20, 21, 22, 24).

The rapid increase in literacy in the sixteenth, seventeenth and eighteenth centuries, not only generated a demand for more books, but also popularized the art of handwriting. Artists, who had previously been engaged in the decoration of books, now turned their skill to the teaching of calligraphy and the production of elaborate instruction manuals. At first these were produced from woodcuts and imitated the effect of a chisel-cut quill. Later the advent of copper engraving, together with the introduction of the flexible steel-pointed pen, made possible a very different form of lettering known as copperplate – and heralded another of the great changes in the design and decoration of letters. The writing masters, of which there were many, vied with each other in demonstrating their highly skilled penmanship by producing elaborate copybooks (plates 25, 26). The majority of printed books, however, retained a classically elegant and austere simplicity and used very little in the way of decoration.

In the nineteenth century the Industrial Revolution triggered off an outburst of creative energy in the design of ornamental letters, helped on to no little extent by the invention of lithography in 1789. The technical possibilities of this new method of printing were exploited to the full in an exuberant flow of ideas and images, some of them bordering on the ridiculous. The need for advertising, brought about by the mass-production capacity of new machinery, encouraged the invention of numerous new alphabets each trying to outdo the other (plates 27, 28, 29). The result sometimes was an unfortunate loss of integrity. This trend, however, was counteracted by a growing interest in antiquities and by the influence of artists such as Henry Shaw and William Morris who, with their careful studies of ancient manuscripts, brought back the importance to the form of the letter itself. Their work, together with the influence of oriental art, paved the way for the sinuous organic forms of *Art Nouveau* (plates 30, 31).

The First World War, however, brought all this to a halt. The 'Gothick' fancies of the nineteenth century were swept away by a wave of functionalism, and ornamentation became unacceptable. Even in the field of letter design a rigid geometricity was imposed, resulting in the fresh and lively style of the *Art Deco*.

The twentieth century has also seen a revival in the art of calligraphy, based largely on the teaching of Edward Johnston. His preoccupation was with the direct use of the chisel-cut pen and an adherence to classical forms with almost no decoration. His influence was worldwide, as is demonstrated by the modern alphabets shown in this book. The easily accessible methods of reproduction available today make it possible for hand-lettering to be used in design work of all sorts, and it is again emerging as a sophisticated and imaginative art form, its very personal image contrasting happily with the uniformity of type and computer lettering. It is interesting to observe that today's lettering artists treat the alphabet as a complete entity: they are not only involved in designing individual letters, but also in presenting the alphabet as one harmonious whole.

Today, decorative lettering is very much part of everyday life; it appears on posters, book jackets, television captions, T-shirts, letterheads, business cards, food packaging, and in graphic work of all descriptions. It can inform and instruct, attract or repel, excite, annoy or intrigue us. Whatever its impact, I hope that the variety of decorative alphabets in this book will give much pleasure, and help to sow the seeds of a multitude of stimulating new ideas whilst being a source of interest and enjoyment for all.

THE POSTER ART SERIES

THE PLATES

FROM THE BRITISH MUSEUM, ROYAL MS. I. E. VI.

PLATE 1

These lovely Anglo-Saxon letters are taken from St Cuthbert's Gospels, now in the British Museum, written in the north-east of England toward the end of the seventh century. A codicil, (a note describing the making of the book), added some 250 years later, tells us that it was written by Aedrith, Bishop of Lindisfarne, 'for God and for St Cuthbert'. These letters were used in the decorated opening pages of each Gospel and to mark the beginnings of new paragraphs. Although some of their forms are unfamiliar to us today, their lively angularity lends them readily to modern interpretation. Their edgings and patterns of little red dots are typical of this period and help to unify the decorative initials with the rest of the page. The ornamental arch is taken from the same manuscript and shows many of the patterns used in Anglo-Saxon decoration; interlacing plaits and knots, stepped designs, spirals, tendrils and strange human and animal heads.

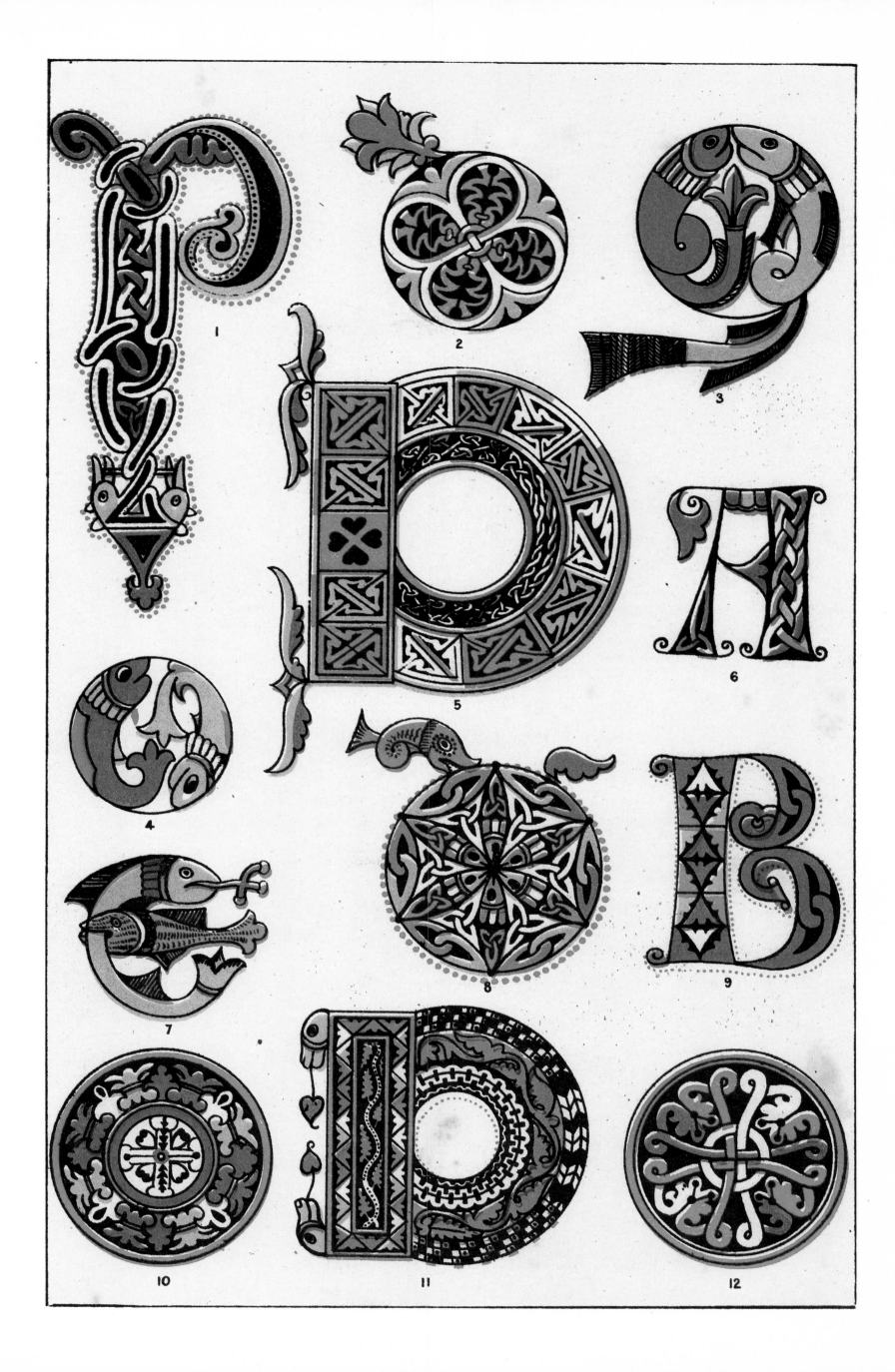

PLATE 2

In the seventh and eighth centuries much use was made of interlacing strapwork decoration combined with strange beasts and fish. These colourful initials come from Spain and show plaited and interlaced work, as well as stylized floral forms. Note how the two fish and their tails are organized to make up the letter 'Q'. There is plenty of simple pattern work here too; the letter 'D' (no. 11) contains at least six different varieties.

PLATE 3

These decorative letters are from a Bible illuminated for Charles the Bald, grandson of the Emperor Charlemagne. The strapwork and curious beasts are highly characteristic of tenth century work. Note how the 'S' is formed from one very strange animal, complete with knotted tail.

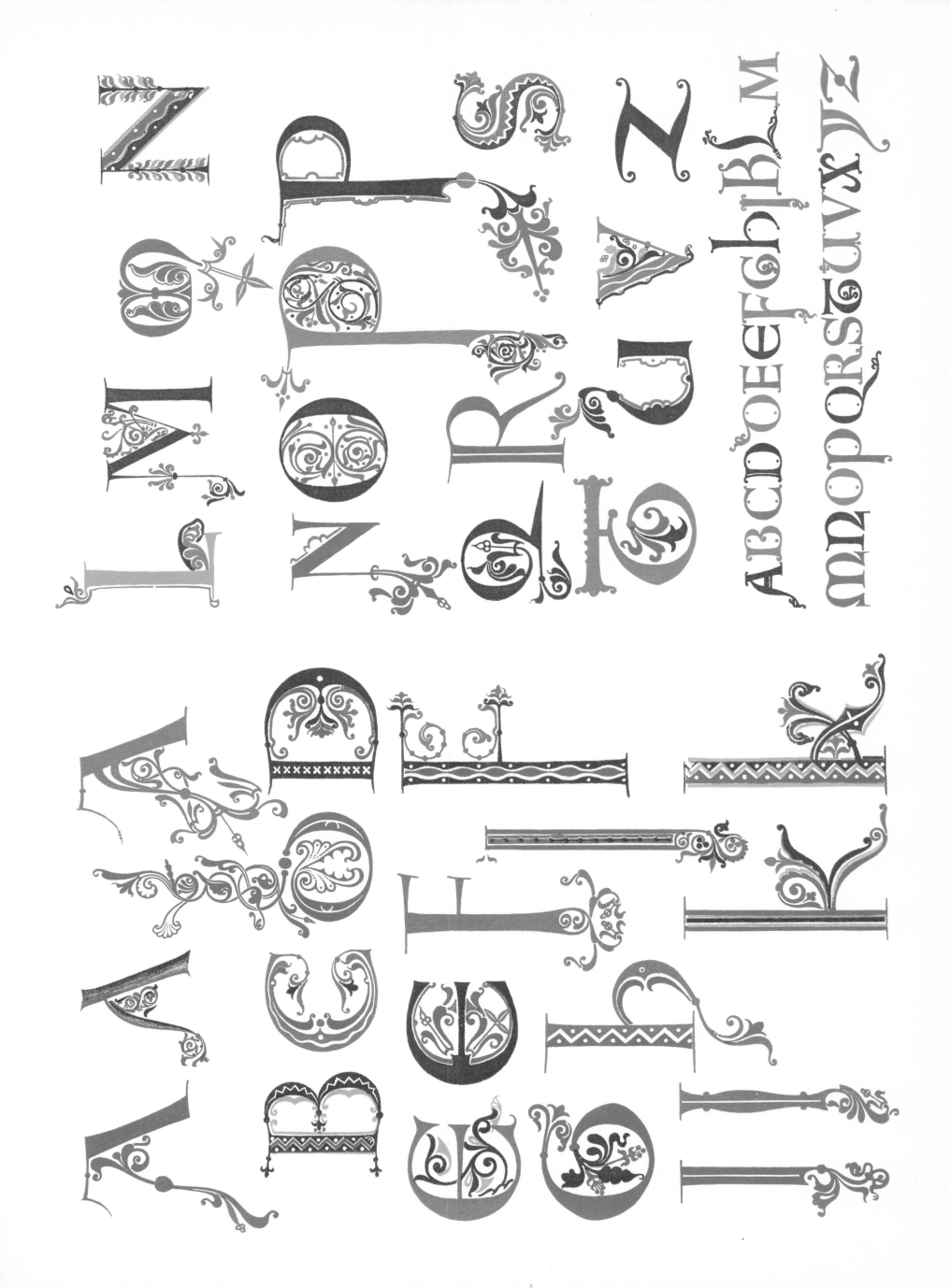

PLATE 4

This alphabet is taken from various twelfth century manuscripts in the British Museum and is the work of the nineteenth century artist Henry Shaw. The classical elegance of these early versals is matched by the restraint of its decoration and the use of simple colouring. The letters sometimes carry basic geometric patterns and are enriched by a variety of formal floral motifs. Note the lively form of the letter 'K' and the design of the 'A's', where the cross bar is omitted, but suggested by the decoration.

PLATE 5

These letters appear to be a playground for dragons and other mythological creatures which leap among formal foliage chasing their own or each other's tails. Nevertheless they present satisfactory and well-balanced patterns, full of vitality. These major illuminated initials came from the same manuscript as many of those in plate 4, and were used to mark important passages, the lesser letters being reserved for the beginnings of verses or paragraphs.

ABCDEF
GHIRLM
NOPQRS
TUVWY
abcdefghijklmno
pqrstuvwxyz

PLATE 6

This capital letter, which is drawn with a pen and then filled in, is a form of versal letter known as Lombardic which was much used throughout the twelfth, thirteenth and fourteenth centuries. The gently concave lines of the sides of the verticals and the pointed outer edges of the curves are the main characteristics of these letters, all of which are easily recognizable to the modern eye. In manuscripts it was used for the beginnings of paragraphs and in lines of capitals for subtitling. In later manuscripts it was often used as an initial in a more distorted and exaggerated form on a burnished gold or highly decorated background.

PLATE 7

These letters come from a manuscript in the British Museum and their austere and spiky forms are typical of work of the thirteenth century. The solid opaque colours of the body of the letter are highlighted with white patterning, usually geometric but with some leaf motifs. Other decoration springs naturally from the letter form and seems to represent a growing shoot rather than a tendril. Each letter is placed on a plain burnished gold background, its sculpted edge following the form of the decoration. Note the use of strong black outlines and of tiny heads as finials to the serifs. The illustration of a monk tasting wine probably has some special local significance, as the use of pictures is unusual in illumination of this period.

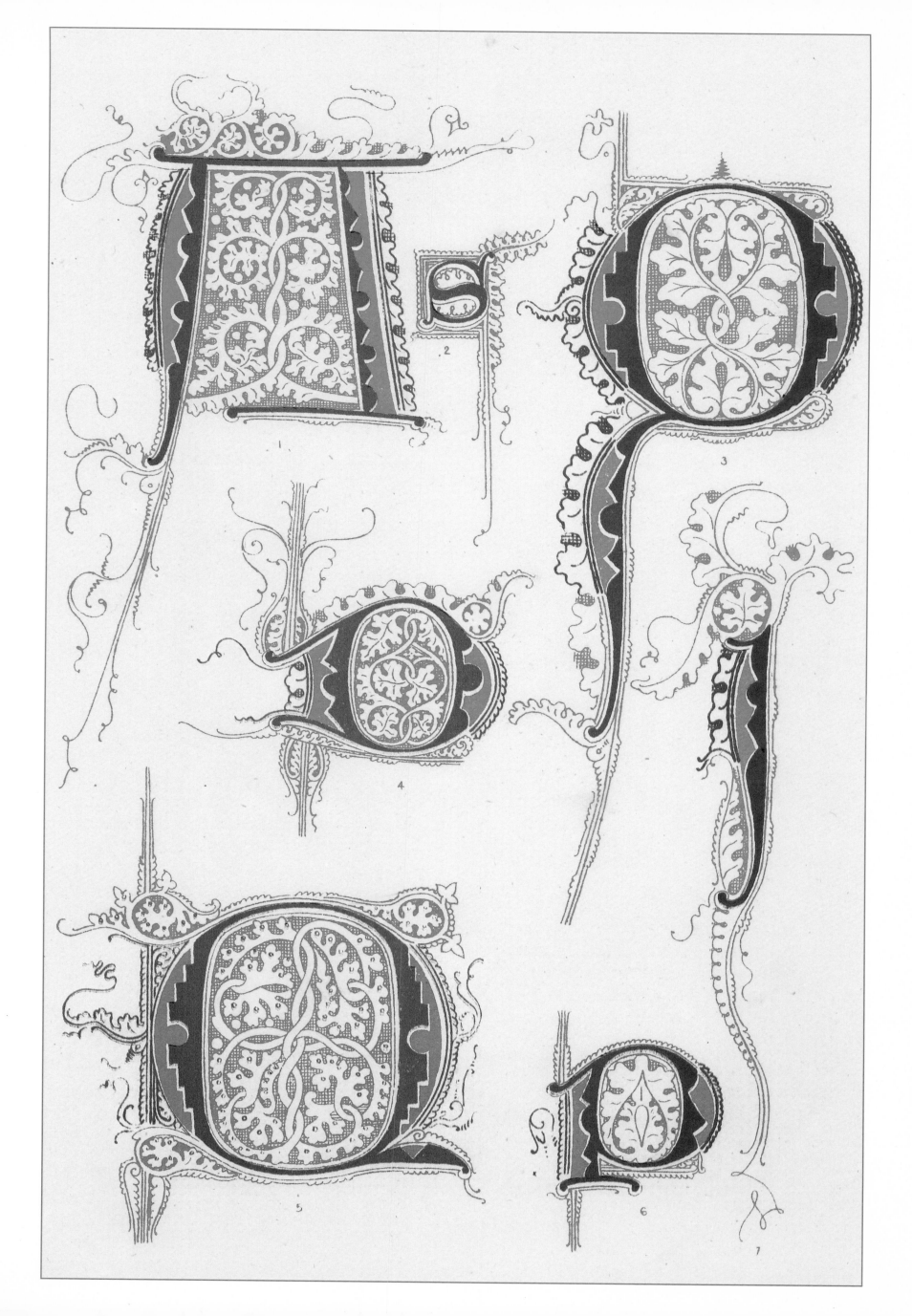

PLATE 8

This page is a wonderful example of the decorative effects that can be achieved by the use of two colours only; the strong, simplified shapes of the letters being emphasized by a sort of counterchange pattern of solid red and blue. Inside each letter is a white design set against a cross-hatched background of red, giving a pink effect. Filigree work and tendrils in red and blue branch out following the lines of each letter, their fine patterning bridging the boldness of the main letters and the page. The crossbar of the 'A' has disappeared and is indicated only by the elongation of the inner serif of the right hand stroke, while the bowl of the 'P' has been so enlarged that the down stroke is almost eliminated and the letter could be mistaken for a 'D'.

1

2

3

4

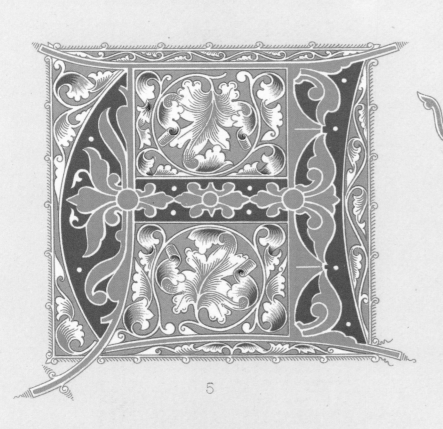

5

6

PLATE 9

The fourteenth century saw the major flowering of the art of the illuminated initial in Europe. The letters are bold and bright, their forms decoratively divided in contrasting colours and the spaces in and around them filled with floral decoration set on a coloured ground. Each letter and its ornamentation forms a solid rectangle of rich pattern and many carry an edging of delicate pen work, important in that it helps to integrate the initial and the page. The centre pair of letters shown here are typical of earlier illumination of the thirteenth century, with their uncomplicated letterforms, formal flowers and angular backgrounds.

PLATE 10

These fourteenth century letters were taken from an embroidered altar cloth in the Church of St Mary at Soest in Westphalia. The letter forms, similar to the Lombardic capitals shown in plate 6, grow ivy or vine leaves from their serifs, and each fits very happily into its diamond-shaped compartment. Note the flowers at the intersection points, and how sometimes these grow their own sprig of leaves in order to fill up the appropriate space. Also interesting is the form of the letters 'S' and 'X', and the way in which one long serif acts for both bars in the letter 'F'.

Date 1385.

From a MS. in the Hunterian Museum, Glasgow.

From the British Museum.

Royal MS. 6 E. IX.

Date about 1330.

PLATE 11

The alphabet at the top of this plate is made up of letters from a late fourteenth century manuscript. They are based on pen-made Gothic capitals, show some alternative forms, and are arranged in a chequerboard design, with red and blue letters on blue and red backgrounds respectively. The filigree lines of the background patterning are cleverly organized so that the effect is of a leaf-like form on a coloured ground. The unexpected way in which some of the letters extend in flourishes beyond their containing squares adds a liveliness to the whole design. Compare this with Sheila Waters' alphabet (plate 35) in which filigree lines are used to quite different effect.

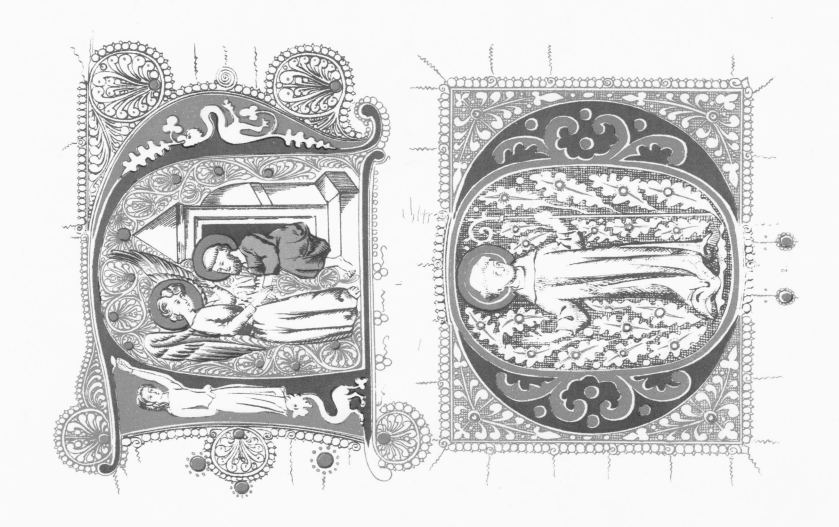

PLATE 12

During the latter part of the fourteenth century, the space inside the letters began to be used for pictorial illustration of the text. In these four examples, taken from manuscripts in the Victoria and Albert Museum, the figures, portraying saints and priests, are set against complicated patterned backgrounds, and the letters themselves are ornamented and surrounded by rectangles of filigree work.

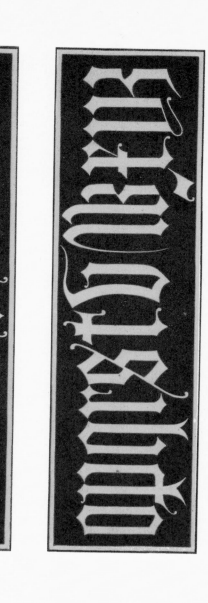

PLATE 13

These alphabets, assembled from lettering on the tomb of Richard II and other contemporary monuments, show a fine version of Gothic lettering. Note the interesting way in which the curves of the letters 'C, E, G, O, and Q' have been treated, adding greatly to their decorative quality but little to their readability. The 'M' also would be difficult to recognize out of context, but the design of the 'S' is highly satisfactory. Also shown are some of the strange grotesques often found in decoration of this period.

PLATE 14

The fifteenth century saw the beginnings of the Renaissance period in Italy and under its influence letterforms once more tended to revert to the classical Roman style. This elegant alphabet is taken from Italian manuscripts and shows delicately proportioned letters, set against filigree backgrounds. Note that alternatives are shown for a number of the letters.

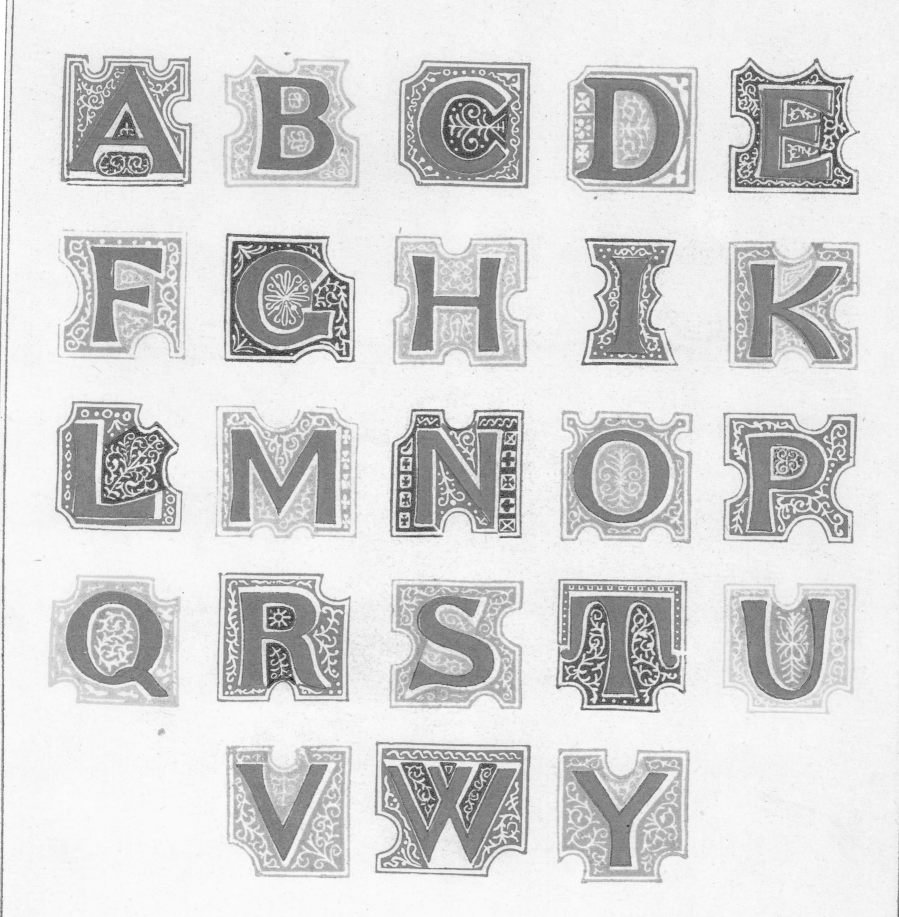

PLATE 15

This alphabet, from a fifteenth century Italian manuscript, shows a heavy version of the Roman letter with almost no serifs and less contrast between the thick and thin strokes than in classical letters. It has, however, a robust charm of its own, each letter being set in a cartouche, or frame of simple filigree work.

PLATE 16

These beautiful Lombardic capitals were taken from a French pattern book of the fifteenth century. Each letter is painted in shaded red or blue, and worked over with patterns in Chinese White. Note that the 'B' and the 'R' carry a ribbon-like motif which may be compared to the use of ribbon designs in plates 18 and 23. The burnished gold backgrounds are ornamented with naturalistic flowers amongst which can be found rose, pansy, strawberry, columbine, wallflower, cornflower, sweet pea, iris and thistle – a veritable cottage garden. Note that the red letters tend to have blue flowers and the blue, red.

PLATE 17

*This sixteenth century initial letter comes
from an illuminated Gregorian chant on
vellum. The classical Roman 'S' is in blue,
marbled in gold, on a gold ground richly
embellished with naturistically painted
flowers. Close inspection, however, reveals
that some liberties have been taken. The red
and blue leaves no doubt were included to
balance the composition.*

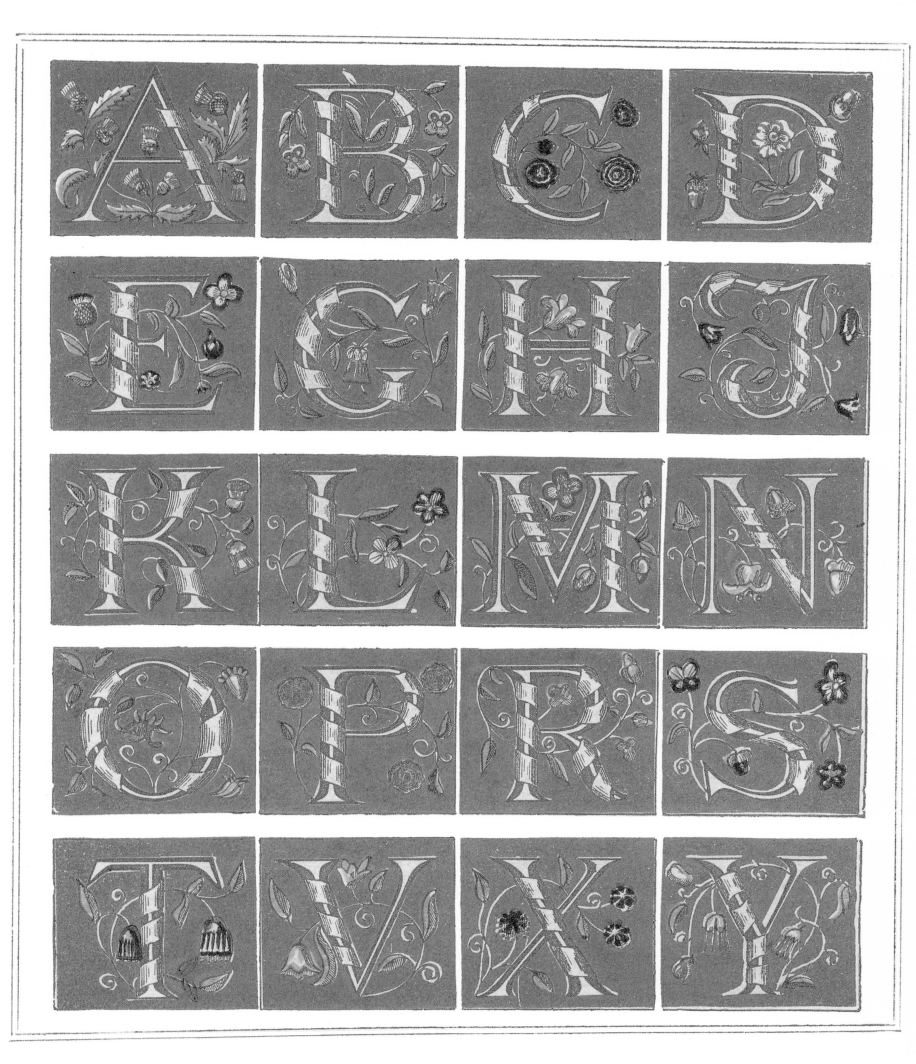

PLATE 18

This alphabet is typical of the sixteenth century illuminated letter produced for use in printed books. The letterform is Roman based, but somewhat clumsily proportioned. It is shown as entwined with ribbons (see also plates 16 and 23) and set in a gold square, decorated with naturalistic flowers. The mauve colouring is typical of this period, though sometimes a delicate shade of pink was substituted. It is interesting to note that this alphabet comes from a nineteenth century instruction book on illuminating, the introduction to which states that the illustrations were exclusively printed from wood blocks.

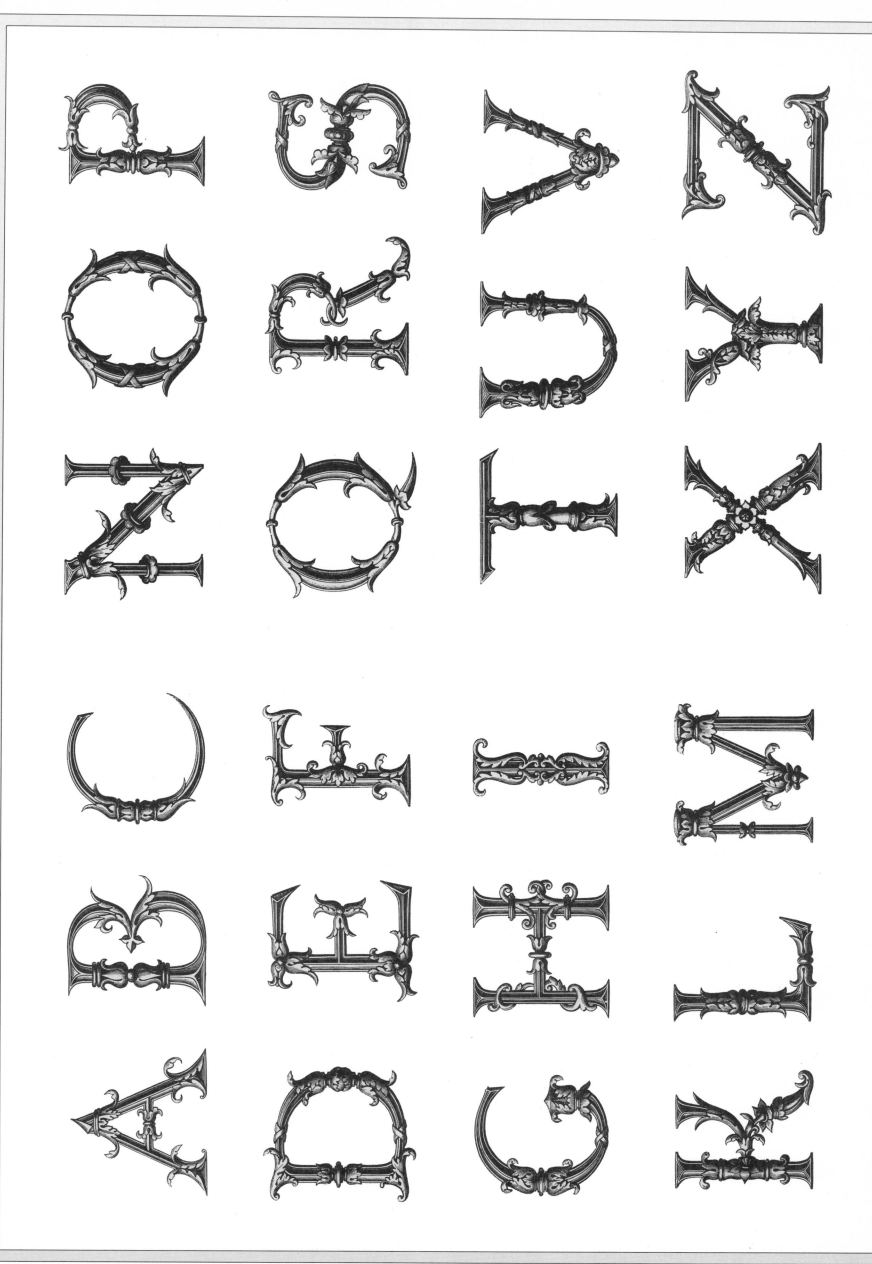

PLATE 19

These letters came from a book, printed on vellum in Milan in 1490 (a presentation copy for Cardinal Sforza), in which the initials were added by hand to the printed page. They were designed as being made up of mouldings joined by decorative foliage and, in the original, were realistically shaded in brown, red, blue or green, highlighted in gold. Each letter was originally placed on an elaborate background of pearls, flowers and scroll work, in the same rich colours.

PLATE 20

Here we have examples of initial letters from a German Bible, printed in Wittenburg in 1584. In the sixteenth century, both in Germany and Italy, elaborate wood engraved initials were freuently used to decorate the printed page, this technique producing a typical white on black effect, and allowing the use of much detail. Here the letter retains its classical Roman proportions but is built up, most imaginatively, of cherubs, beasts, flowers, scrolls, vases and moulded forms, together achieving a unity out of their very diversity.

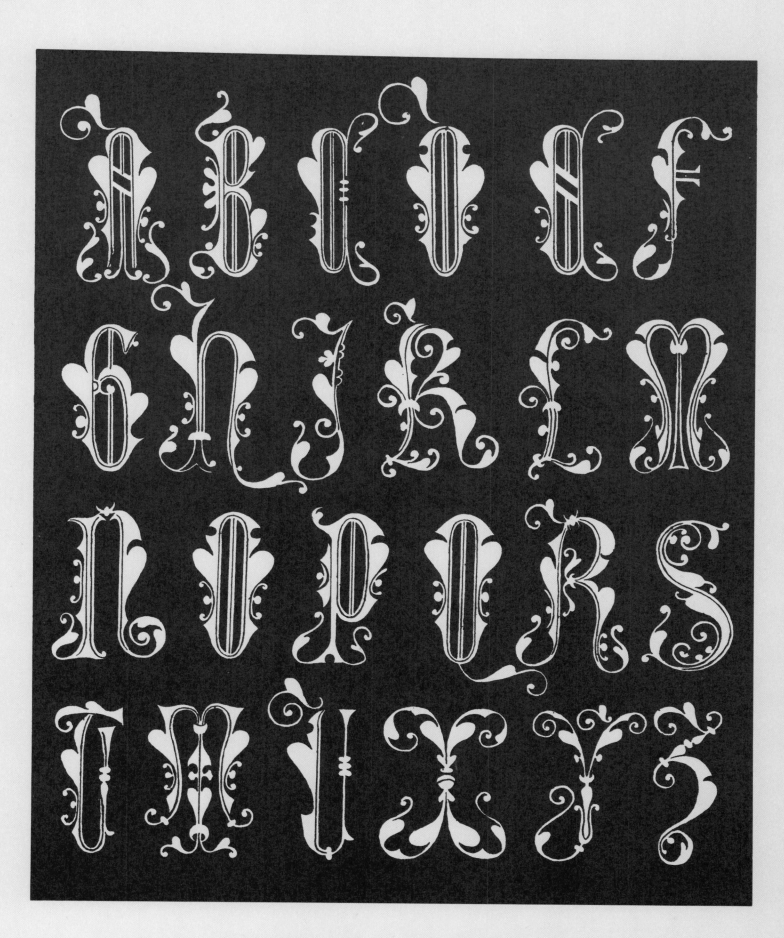

XVITH CENT. ITALIAN.

PLATE 21

These intriguing letters were probably designed in Venice in the late sixteenth century. The structure of each letter has been distorted and elaborated, but almost all are recognizable to us today, the exceptions being the 'D' and 'E' and the 'K' which could be mistaken for an 'R'. Note the central division of the counter, or interior space in many of the letters, the complex swelling of the lines, and the graceful tendrils. Compare these with the ornate alphabet shown in plate 22.

PLATE 22

These letters are derived from a manuscript in the Bayerische Staatsbibliothek, Munich. The nineteenth century book from which this plate is reproduced dates them as of the twelfth century, but they are more probably of the fifteenth or sixteenth. An extremely complicated alphabet with both straight and swelling lines and elaborate scrolls and tendrils, its most telling characteristic is the use of dots, both open and solid. Note also the unusual form of the letter 'S' where the tail is extended to form the upper curve of the letter.

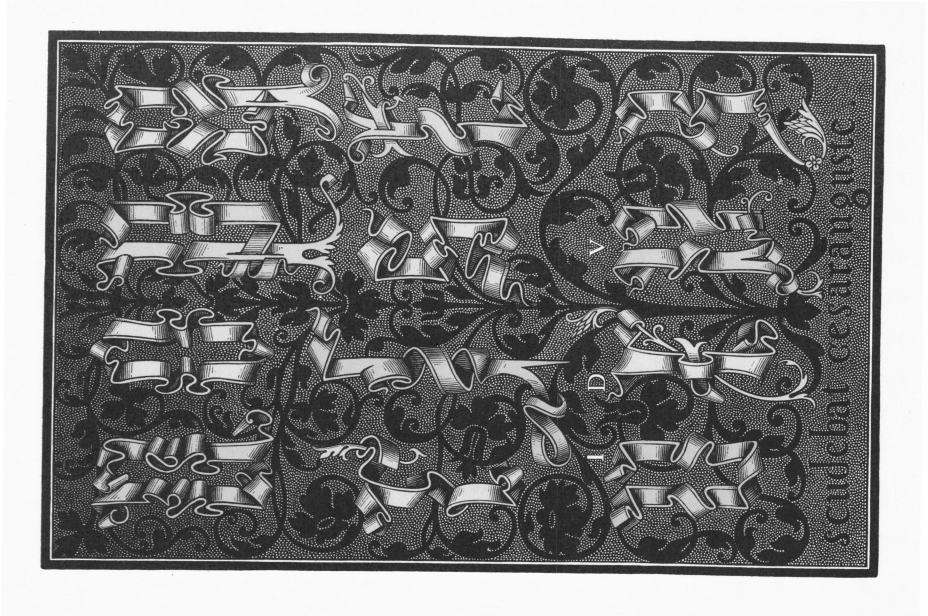
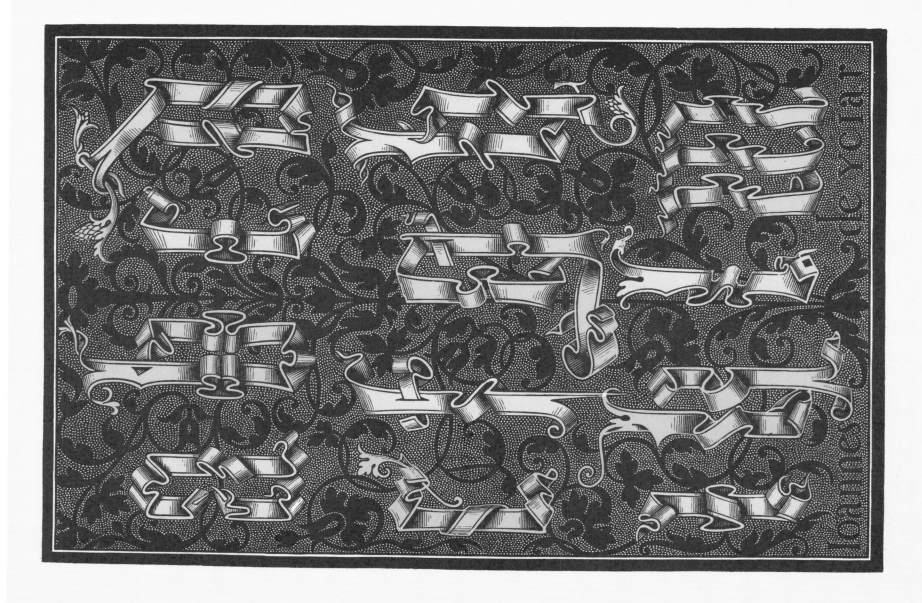

PLATE 23

These fascinating letters are drawn as if constructed of pleated and folded ribbon. Designed by Juan de Yciar in Spain in the middle of the sixteenth century, they were engraved on wood by his collaborator, Jean de Vingle and included in his important book The Subtle Art of Teaching a Perfect Hand *published in Saragossa in 1550.*

PLATE 24

Henry Shaw, the nineteenth century artist, took these letters from the Missale Trajectense *and other manuscripts of the mid and late fifteenth century. Their white on black character shows their origin in wood engraving, while the interlaced structure of the letters derives from tenth century manuscripts. (See plates 2 and 3). They are decorated with beautifully drawn flower and leaf motifs except for the 'O' which carries a face surrounded by scroll work probably representing the sun. Note also the shape of the 'M', so designed to fit comfortably into its square.*

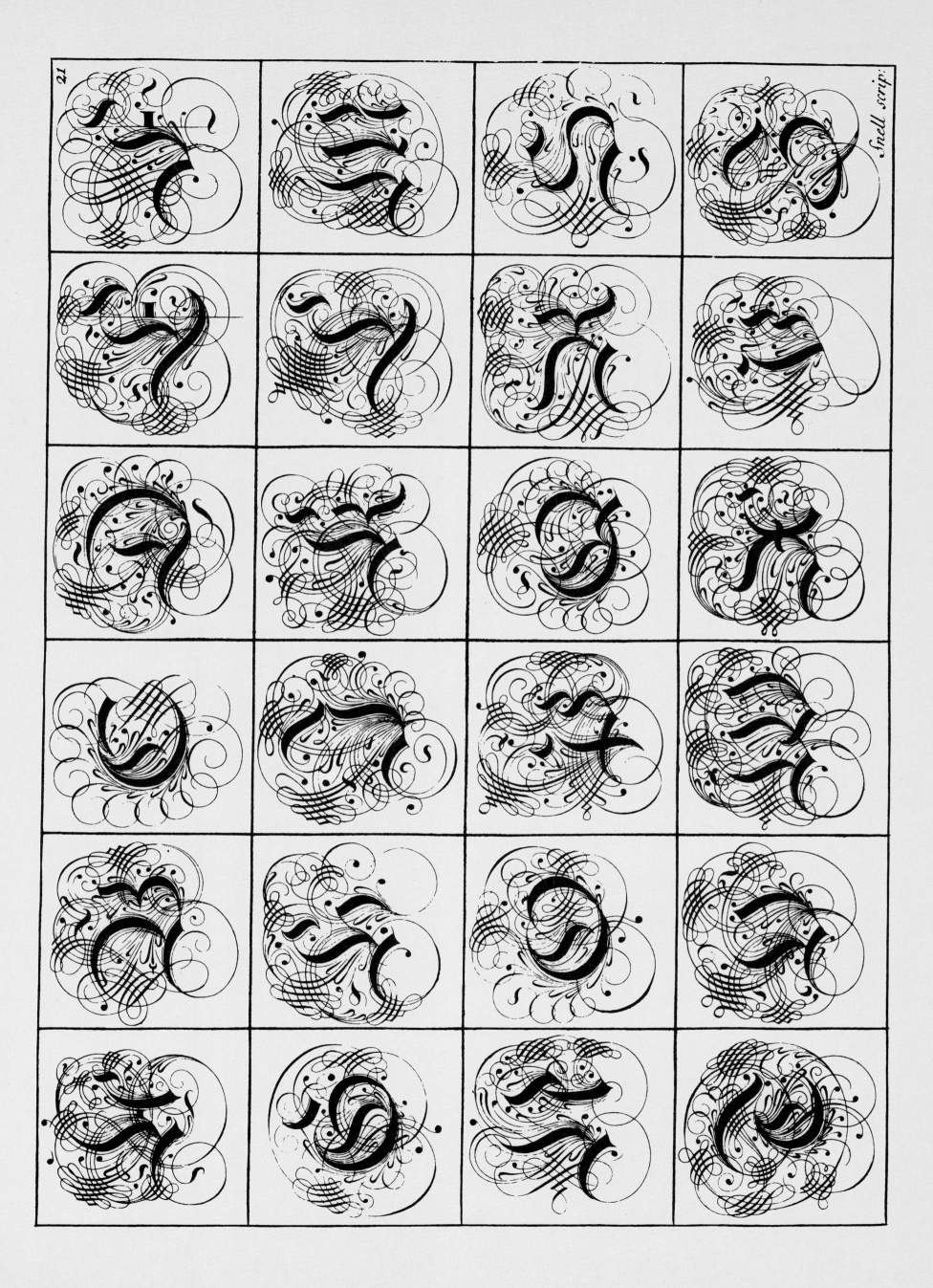

PLATE 25

During the seventeenth and eighteenth centuries, book design became more austere and we have to look to the writing masters of the time for examples of decorative letters. Charles Snell published his The Pen-man's Treasury Open'd, *from which this alphabet comes, in 1693. It is subtitled* A New Essay for the Improvement of Free and Natural Writing in ye English, French and Italian Hands. *This page is a* tour de force *and shows a lively Gothic capital, surrounded by a plethora of fine scrolls, flourishes and interlaced patterns. One cannot help but feel that the 'free and natural writing' of the sub-title is here somewhat of a misnomer.*

Reproduced by permission of the Bodleian Library, Oxford.

Neither praise nor dispraise yourself, your actions serve.

One Ounce of Discretion is more worth yⁿ a Pound of wit.

Pain wasts the Body as pleasures do yͤ Understanding.

Questions of great moment require deliberate Answers.

Rely not on another for what you can do yourself.

Security is commonly the forerunner of great Calamity.

They who are unwilling to mend hate to be Instructed.

Vulgar Persons generally form a wrong Judgment.

Whoever looks not before will soon find himself behind.

Youth commended Vice and Virtuous Exercises.

You cannot expect Glory but in the way of Virtue &c

Zeal for Religion cannot warrant cruelty & wrong

Approve not of him, who commends all you say.

Bestow in chusing a friend, slower in changing.

Conceal your wants from yͫ who cannot help you.

Deride not Infirmities nor insult over Miseries.

Envy is always waiting, where virtue flourishes.

Flattering friends are worse than open Enemies.

Great receipts render us liable to great Accompts.

Humility makes great men twice Honourable.

It is better to take many Injuries yⁿ to give one.

Knowledge of ourselves requires great penetration.

Laziness is commonly punished with Poverty.

Make not a jest at another mans Infirmity.

Shelley scr. 1712

PLATE 26

In the eighteenth century the introduction of the steel-pointed pen had a great influence on the shapes of letters. The flexible nib facilitated the formation by controlled pressure of finely graduated thicks and thins and complex cursive lines. The technique was akin to that of engraving on copper, and this style of writing is therefore generally known as copperplate. This example by George Shelley from a copybook published by George Bickham in 1731 obviously serves two purposes, allowing the student to absorb moral advice whilst practising his penmanship. Note the use of 'y' in place of 'th'.

Reproduced by permission of the Victoria and Albert Museum, London.

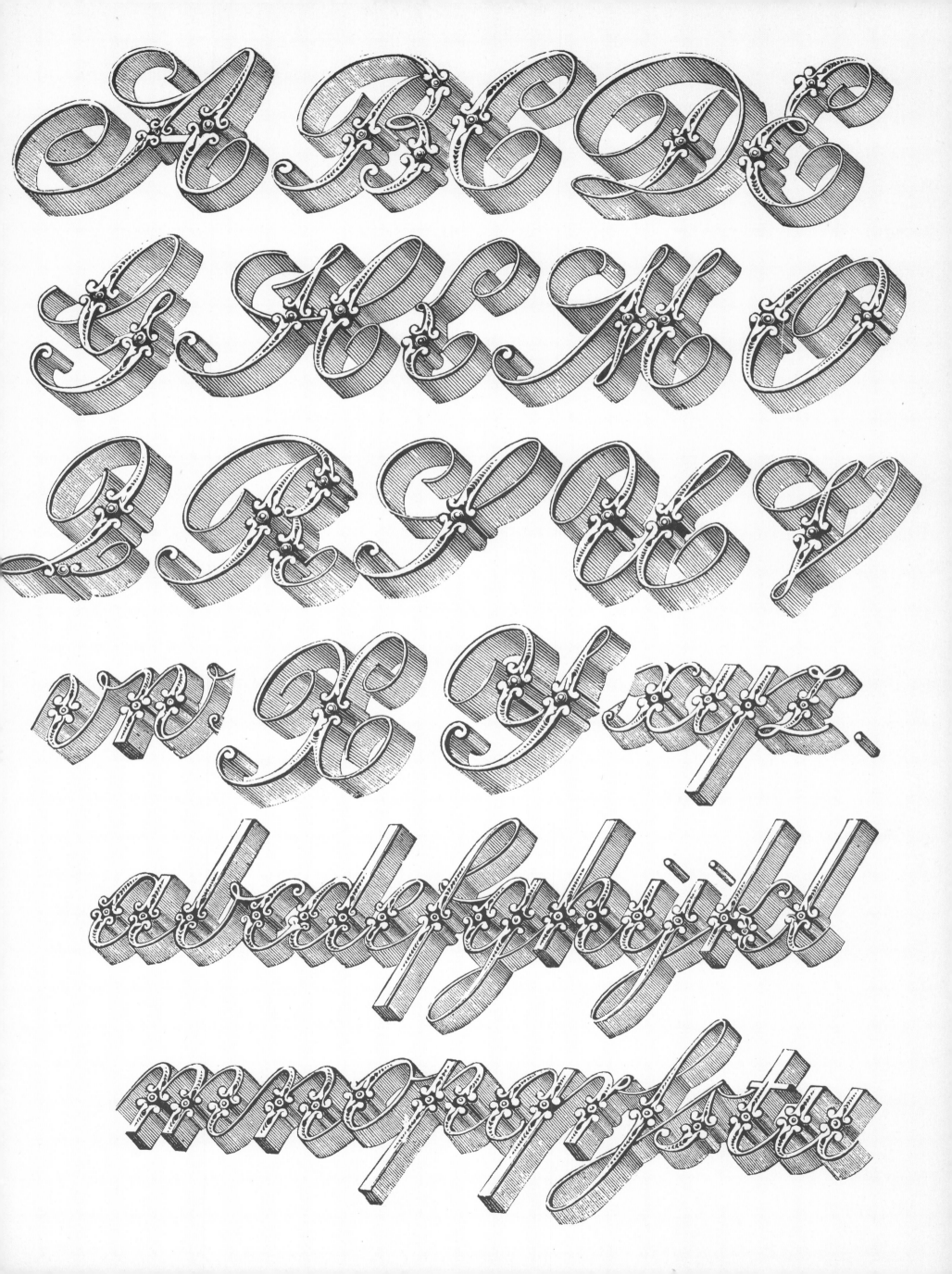

PLATE 27

Decorative lettering reached a peak of variety and invention during the nineteenth century. Here we have a copperplate letter – with its flowing curves and loops embellished with a central decorative motif – made to look as if it formed the edges of a ribbon or strip of metal. This three-dimensional effect was much in use during the Victorian period.

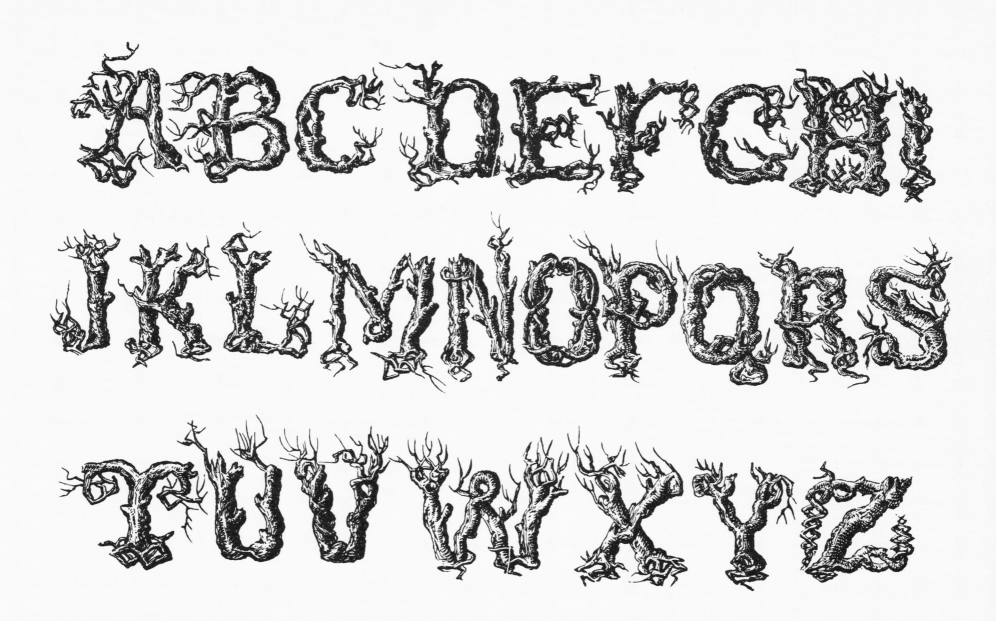

A B C D E F G H
I J K L M N O P Q R S
T U V W X Y Z

a b c d e f g h i j k l m n
o p q r s t u v w x y z
1 2 3 4 5 6 7 8 0 0

PLATE 28

In a great number of Victorian decorative alphabets frequent use was made of twigs, trees and branches which came under the category of 'Rustic' motifs. In this example, tree trunks, roots and bare branches have all been put to use. Close inspection will reveal even here twisting and interlacing patterns, reminiscent of much earlier times.

ARNDT ARGENSON BUFFON.BOSSUET CICÉRON DAGUESSEAU.

   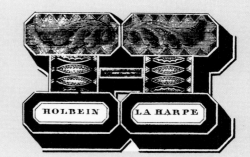

ESMENARD. FLORIAN.FOY GOETHE HOLBEIN LA HARPE

 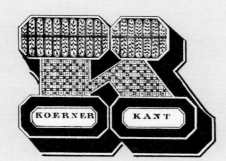  

JACOBI KOERNER KANT LAHARPE.LEIBNITZ Mozart MEIERBEER

Nicolai Newton OBERLIN PERRAULT QUINAULT

   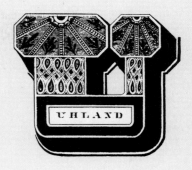

RABELAIS Rossini SCHILLER.SAUL LE TASSE UHLAND

VEGA XIMENES XENOPHON YOUNG.YRIARTE ZSCHOKKE.ZEA

PLATE 29

This alphabet called Lapidaire Monstre *is by the French type designer J. Midolle, and perhaps reaches the ultimate in letter decoration. The bold letterforms with their heavy serifs are divided horizontally into three parts; the two upper sections contain a wide variety of all-over patterns, some geometric and some floral in origin, while for good measure the lower parts carry the surnames of famous men which correspond to each letter. It is nevertheless a useful alphabet in that it lends itself to adaptation and is an inspiring source of infilling designs.*

ABCDEFGHI
JKLMNOPQR
STUVWXYZ

A

BCDEF
GHIJK
LMNOP
QRSTU
VWXYZ

Ch. Mulier, déco.   Ch. Juliot, Éditeur, Dourdan (Set 6)   Monrocq, Imp. Paris

PLATE 30

The elegance of the Art Nouveau *period makes a refreshing change from the excesses of the Victorian era. The letters shown here are good examples of the controlled fluidity of line associated with this style, and are the work of the French artist E. Mulier. Developed during the last years of the nineteenth century* Art Nouveau *flourished during the early part of this century, but did not survive the First World War.*

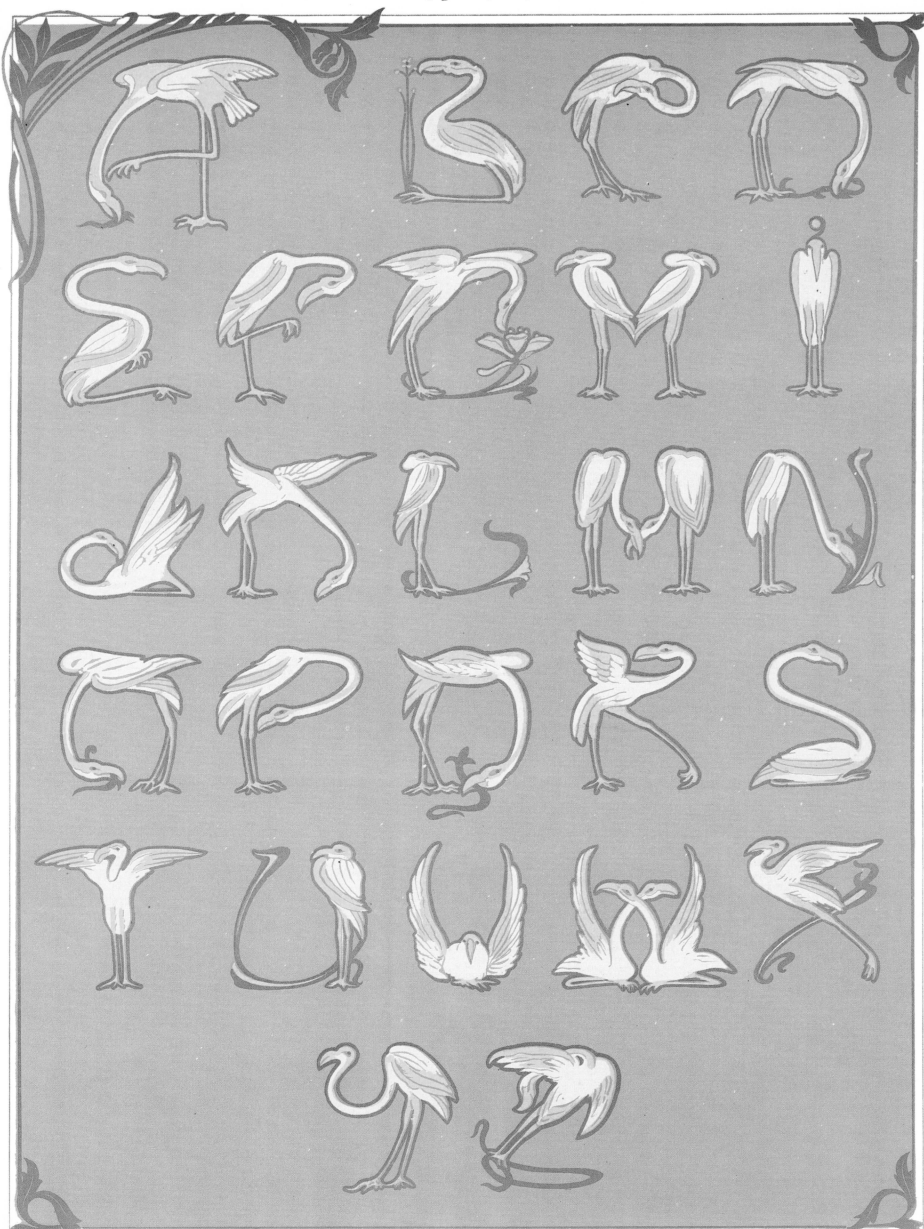

PLATE 31

Typically Art Nouveau *in style, this witty alphabet manipulates the sinuous form of the flamingo in order to create unusual letters, some of which would be difficult to recognize out of context.*

110 MORNINGSIDE DRIVE · NEW YORK CITY · **(212) 666 · 3738**

PRINTED BY WATER STREET PRESS 1986

PLATE 32

Although designed in 1986, Paul Shaw's alphabet is characteristic of the trends which followed the First World War in that the bold shapes of his letters reflect the functionalism and geometric precision of the Art Deco *style. As with other modern lettering artists, however, he has designed his alphabet as a single entity, with the letters not so much considered as separate units but as elements making up a whole. Note the dry brush form of the letter 'S' which he uses as a signature in his work. Paul Shaw is a free-lance calligrapher and graphic artist who also teaches at several universities and art schools in the New York area.*

PLATE 33

This work by John Smith is entitled Alphascape; *it consists of the letters of the alphabet, together with the word 'alphabet' and the letters 'E' and 'T' freely drawn in a mixture of capitals and lower case letters and arranged to build up a satisfying composition. The artist uses transfer mechanical tints to emphasize some of the shapes and the colour has been added by hand. He says that he is fascinated by the permutations of shapes and spaces created by the twenty six letters and by the endless potential of the playing of the positive against the negative. John Smith is a lettering artist who works and teaches in Britain.*

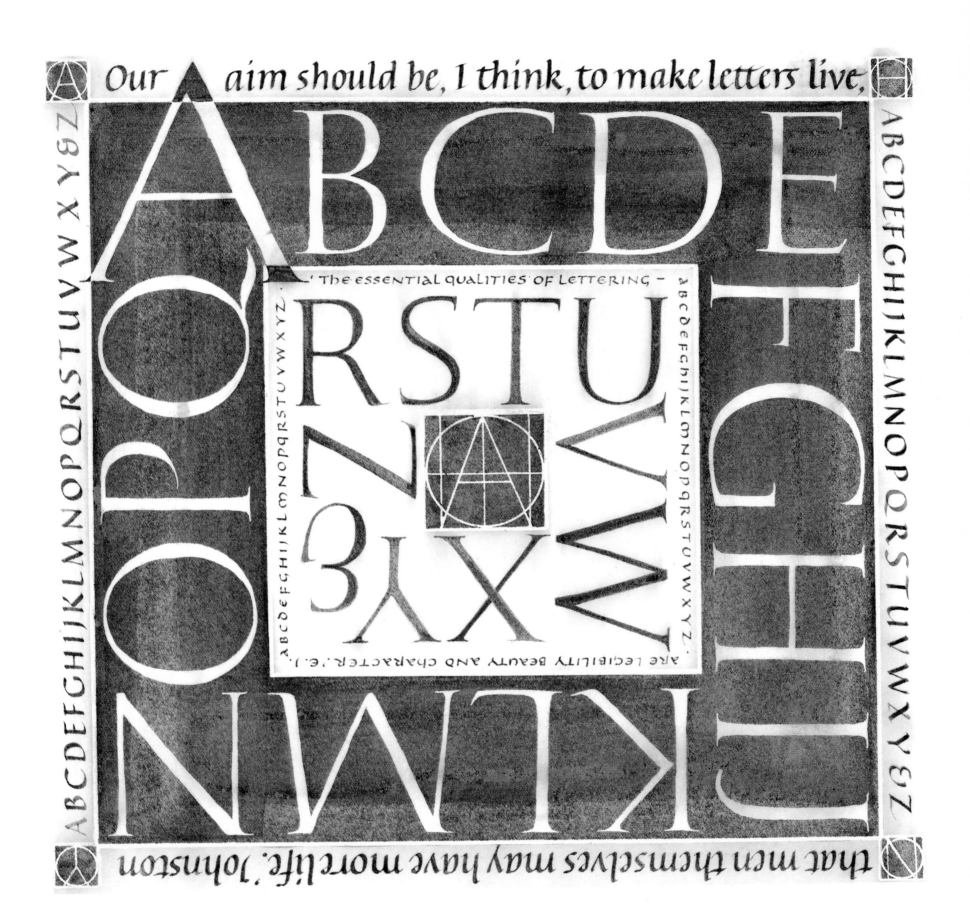

Our aim should be, I think, to make letters live; that men themselves may have more life.' Johnston

PLATE 34

The letter used in this alphabet was developed by the Romans in the first century A.D. and its fine proportions and logical design have made it the standard form for classical lettering ever since. Here Anne Irwin uses it to great decorative effect by clever arrangement and colouring. The borders of alphabets and quotations from Edward Johnston's writings not only add interest, but also serve to integrate the letter with its background. Anne Irwin is a calligrapher who lives and works in London.

Quotation from Edward Johnston's Formal Penmanship *is by permission of Lund Humphries Publishers Ltd, London.*

Quotation from Edward Johnston's Writing and Illuminating Lettering *is by permission of Pitman Publishing Ltd, London.*

PLATE 35

This fine alphabet, with its strong letter-forms and delicately drawn decoration, is the work of Sheila Waters, an internationally known calligraphic artist working in the U.S.A. Her letters are based on Roman proportions, although the 'A' and the 'E' in this example show an Anglo-Saxon influence (see plate 1). Note the strength given to the design by the fusing of some of the letters, for example – L to M, T to U and Y to Z. Although the ornamentation seems to echo work of previous centuries, Sheila Waters has here produced a unique work of art, one of the finest of its genre.

Peter Halliday

PLATE 36

This example shows a combination of two different pen-made alphabets. The red letter is a very freely written form of Roman capital using a five line pen. This is superimposed on a blue alphabet of uncials based on a study of the text letter in St Cuthbert's Gospels in the British Museum (see plate 1). The artist Peter Halliday is a calligrapher working and teaching in Britain.

PLATE 37

This modern alphabet by Jean Larcher is of Gothic capitals loosely based on the type of lettering found in German manuscripts of the fourteenth and fifteenth century. Much of its decorative quality comes from the use of double pen strokes, the freedom of the arrangement, and the use of bright colours on a gold and silver ground. Like many Gothic capitals, some of the letters may not be familiar to us out of context – the 'A' for instance, can be confusing, and the 'K' and the 'R' indistinguishable from each other. (See plates 10 and 25 whose letterforms use the same base).

Jean Larcher is internationally known typographic designer and calligrapher who works and teaches in France.

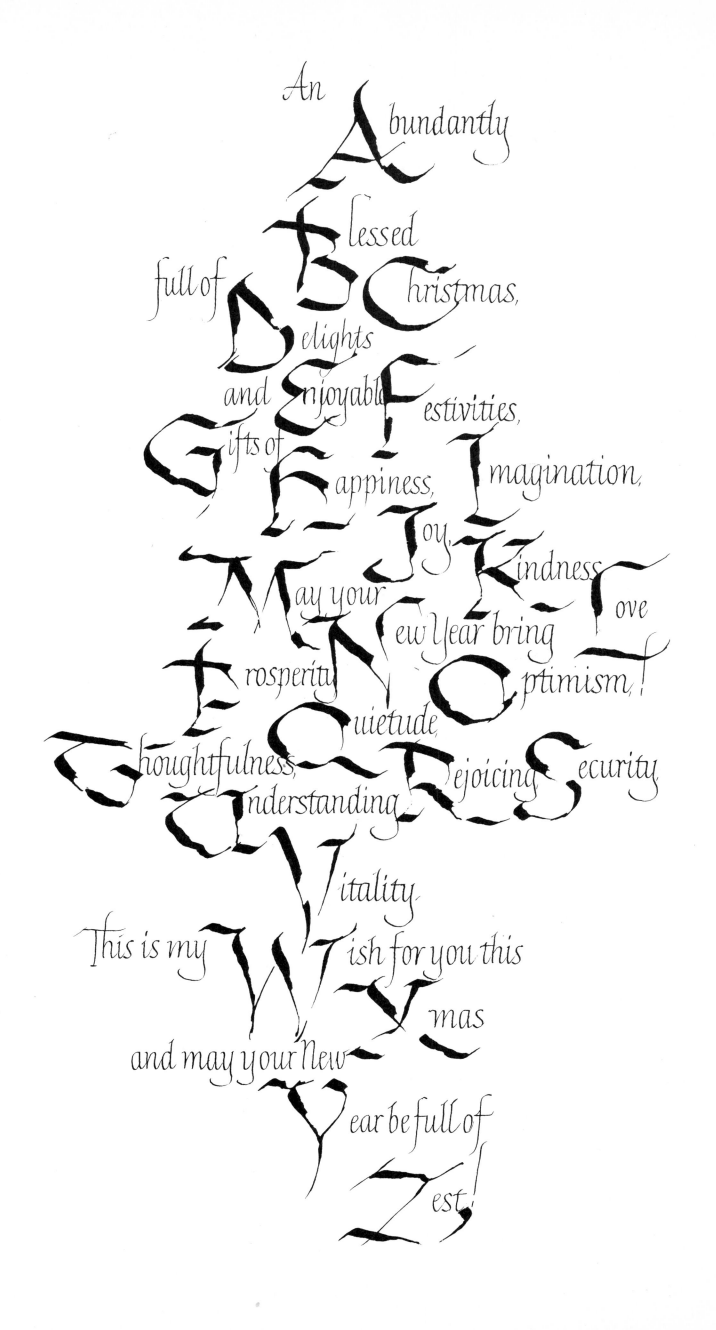

An Abundantly
Blessed
full of Christmas,
Delights
and Enjoyable Festivities,
Gifts of
Happiness, Imagination,
Joy,
Kindness
May your Love
New Year bring
Prosperity Optimism,
Quietude,
Thoughtfulness, Rejoicing Security
Understanding
Vitality
This is my Wish for you this Xmas
and may your New
Year be full of
Zest!

PLATE 39

This Alphabet of Good Wishes *was designed by Pat Russell as her Christmas card in 1986. The freely written Roman capitals owe their ragged appearance to a deliberate twisting and lifting of the pen on the down strokes, the unexpected broken line adding vitality to the letter form. The snowstorm effect on the side lettering was achieved by spattering the double stroke letters with Process White.*

PLATE 40

In this work by Pat Russell scissors and coloured tissue paper have been used to create an unusual alphabet. The cut-paper technique has obviously very much influenced the design of the letters and some very unexpected forms have appeared. Note how similar shapes recur in the letters 'B, C, D, G, K, M, S and X,' and how use has been made of the contrast between the thick and thin, and between the colours. This method of designing allows for great freedom, both in the structure of the letters and in their arrangement. In the background is an alphabet of flowing yellow lines made by using the ink straight from the nozzle of the dispenser.